Arthat ~ Mystic Poetry

Janit Gambhir

Art : Vaiishnavi Ramesh.

Janit Gambhir.

A SOOT imprint, India. 2022

A dancing flame poised like shining eyes. Travelled, unravelled yet unrivalled of tenor.

A grace underscored, approachable to earnest implored.

The flight of constance, clued to faithful lores.

Time tasked with safekeeping of notes in the intonation of sighs.

Memory's lines tucked neatly in the crevices of kindly eyes.

Twice-defined like aged humour in cracks of creaky muscle inclines.

With the quickness of insular warmth, settled with the content of creation and the contentment of perspective's exuberance.

Heartened to insight, when hemmed to wings in vision, and humming hymns of sentiment and deliverance to its sentience.

Like a penchant of prose conning the connotations
from horizons' height.

Heightened to awareness all the same, sky to surmise.

A day in the sun, its night to entwine.

Like dusty letters stretching sublime their agility to
break character grazing past syllables in soliloquy.

The consonant of you, awe gushed wherewithal's
grammar to emote.

Like the clouds, walking on sunshine, and grateful for
allusions nigh.

~   *   ~

Serenade, said the song to the wind.

You found heaven for me. The gates concealed as they were, to my existence until the point of you in revelation.

Now, sight itself wears me in its vernacular, and wonder wrapping the formless to every shape and size to my cognition.

You put me together as if strewn prior to your perception.

The sheen unravels for me a light I knew not to seek out, besmirched as I in own lofty suppositions.

Astound is indeed an easy consort to your appropriation.

This starlit path, as it were, like a birdsong harmonising to a beacon to lend an air. Stardust weaving a glimmering trail of hums elevating in echoes of easing continuums.

The communion of form upon your insight, the dazzle reflecting the sudden burst of peeling joy to existential might. To channel yet the currents that would replete the streams of your aspiration to the consciousness of derived notions. That which you grace.

Whispers of love to your very trace.

Like following the senses to their elation, and find there healed the very fabric in exhilaration. As with the breath inspired in your safekeeping. Gently holding up the world beyond purview, where the mere emotion of you makes a clearing.

Insofar endearing and nearing. Lighting up my universe through your eyes.

You found heaven for me, you beside.

~

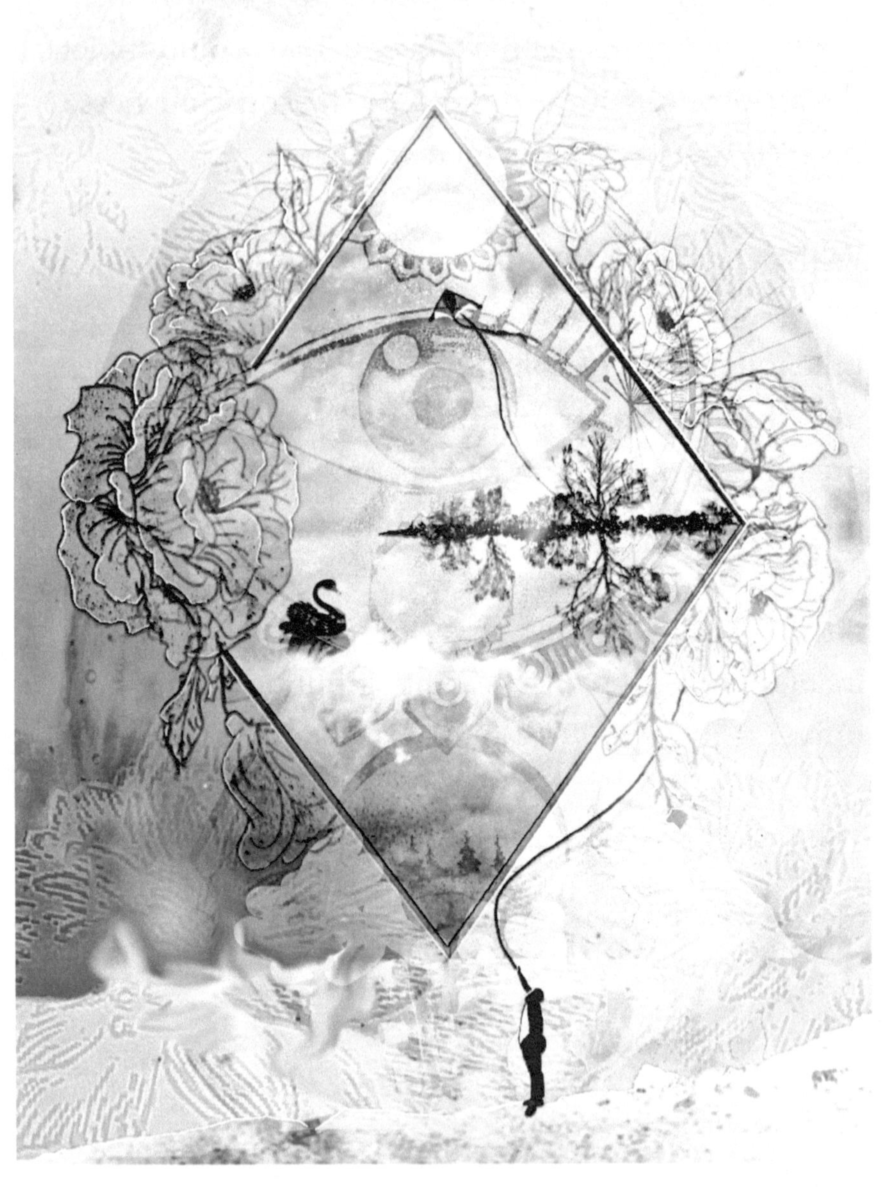

Words that scribe, like translating the falling of rain, that need not surmise.

Ask Square

It isn't an active process, more like a lens that you can either process through, or not, in which case all your words will simply dance around an image, like a dervish grasping the moon as if it were a song.

Like the room that you ruminate in, the other side of the door being all the knowledge accumulated and borrowed from active seeking. Whereas the window always overlooks experience, and is lit in the sunlight of personal history.

Now this square, turned ever so slightly with the eyes. It is always a personal attest, for it is through this upon finding peace, the light from the anchor in the sky comes in.

The encircling relationship with the square is our approach to ourselves, true north and due east, cascading as a question's axis to define us.

When processed, this little square bestows images,
clearer than ordinary imagination, and to purpose then
if pursued.

This is the aspect of fire. One side of the square. And
always subjective. Cut to size, each in his own larger
than life.

A token of substance, a fragment of the self.
Like a broken parchment magnetised to
meaning.

Set in motion to the ache of the soul.
Renewed if only found,
this burst of liveliness, in order to be whole.

A seeker instilled, with rapture of magic.
Conjured and claimed, enigma called to karma.

All of it, as is nectar to be.
The spark in itself saw the flame,
the flame flickered towards…

Filled from within, so as to never be without.

Yet in the silence,
to see is to light up blanks
and fulfil spaces that would erstwhile be
restive to thought.

You cannot trap a shadow, yet you can catch yourself from casting it.

L ines in the sand, cascades of time etched of
reflections making amends.

A beautiful earnest, an endearing past
memory held affectionately to inflect.

The elusive moment that illuminated. Summoned in
mercy of all those that contemplated.

Bridges built notwithstanding, waves to contend.
Onwards and upwards yet, an order emerged.

A sequence for the seeker, an imbalance of doubt,
purged.

Whereupon relevance, a consequence of meaning.
Unconcerned, an objective gathered to feeling.

Awakened to intuition, whence appeared.
De-constructed apparition, clarity neared.

The wheel of motion, spun. Fabric of learning weaved hence. Attention in shapes and sounds healed where so and however bloomed upon, to know instance.

To seek is to be found.

~

Crown of awareness

Goodwill in the shadows. Whispers and hymns of hallow.

The self awake and as if in a dream. Sojourning the senses entwined from within the seams.

But the majestic makes as breath to a divine namesake. Regaled to its own, like stories made to be shown.

In tune and intuited to repose. A calming keepsake conjuring itself awake.

A consolidation of form.

Tipped upon the zodiac's edge piercing the sky at midheaven. Claiming the miracle as if it were the privilege of the mystery.

The contention of mastery, not quite the contest of fools but contending for the mantle of chance in favour.

As if by magic, said the precision to focus.

A wishing well as a wellspring of joy.

Yet tucked away as a cornerstone of the eyes.

A sparkle that would make larger than life seem almost slight.

In that blessing, be. Human, as the err, ergo profound enough to understand itself.

Unlearning and wholesome to the point.

nward the path leads through the skies. The right of way, the manner and nature of thought.

With every breath, the vision is clearer.

The token of devotion imbibed, is that something has to be taken on faith. That is the uncertainty the spirit embraces.

The Ingenuity of the soul set to the resistance of the personality's prejudices. In that understanding is a sentient map, bridged by motivations such as memory, rationality, self-fortification and the like in forms of affinity. What then are words to do, but spark in friction and fold, the semblance of inner fire. The perchance of vision, that each in their worthiness and claim contest.

To move freely the world of will and set about their own boundaries to the universe. That then moves the mind, and within it all images of rendition, are confined.

The act of cognition is divine. Consciousness

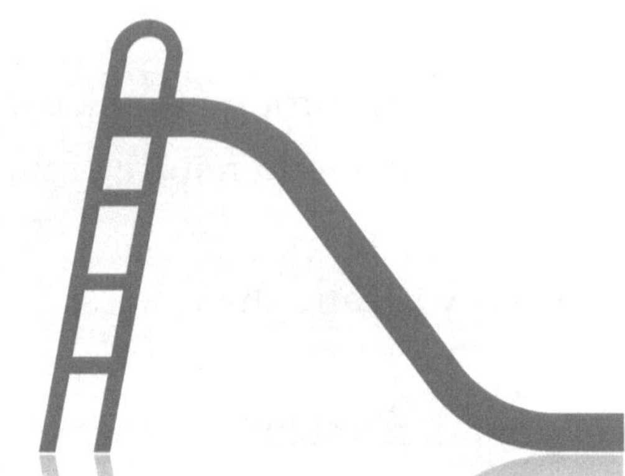

simultaneously the experiencing subject and the object.

Do you see me?

All roads lead into darkness by night and into the horizon by day.

form to adhere. Trying to fit the circle where should be a square.

Information. Like light travelling through the eyes. All over the colour map. Like atlas when the work of giants could be poised to rest.

To triangle as if in rhetoric. If just to fit stardust in an idea bubble. And out of a syllabus of syllables in reverie.

A wave that sets you sailing into a smile.

The attribute.

The softening, like the eyes making for summoning, an answered prayer to your by-coming.

An interstellar purport.

In all seen to your infectious swoon. Histories revisited and rested upon in altering planetary platoons.

Soon to sunshine liken dawn's promising attune.

Deeper colours pitter at the night's palette of black to invite.

Richer in hues, delights the palatial reverb in perspective's enthuse.

Like daylight prancing around a lit lamp's windy fortune to dance.

Shadows of understanding lurking behind, catching up to citing instance.

Reposed and poised, like the familiar in tricks of light to chance.

Mere a moment, in a pause to enhance.

Attribute of you, to you, a second encircling. The winded path of life to your point of comprehension.

A passing crosswords in a cross-roads of densities.

Climbing consciousness with the clarity of your perception. A pinnacle drop to the flights of your reception.

A healer's sphere in your earthly reflection. Here, unto you.

~ * ~

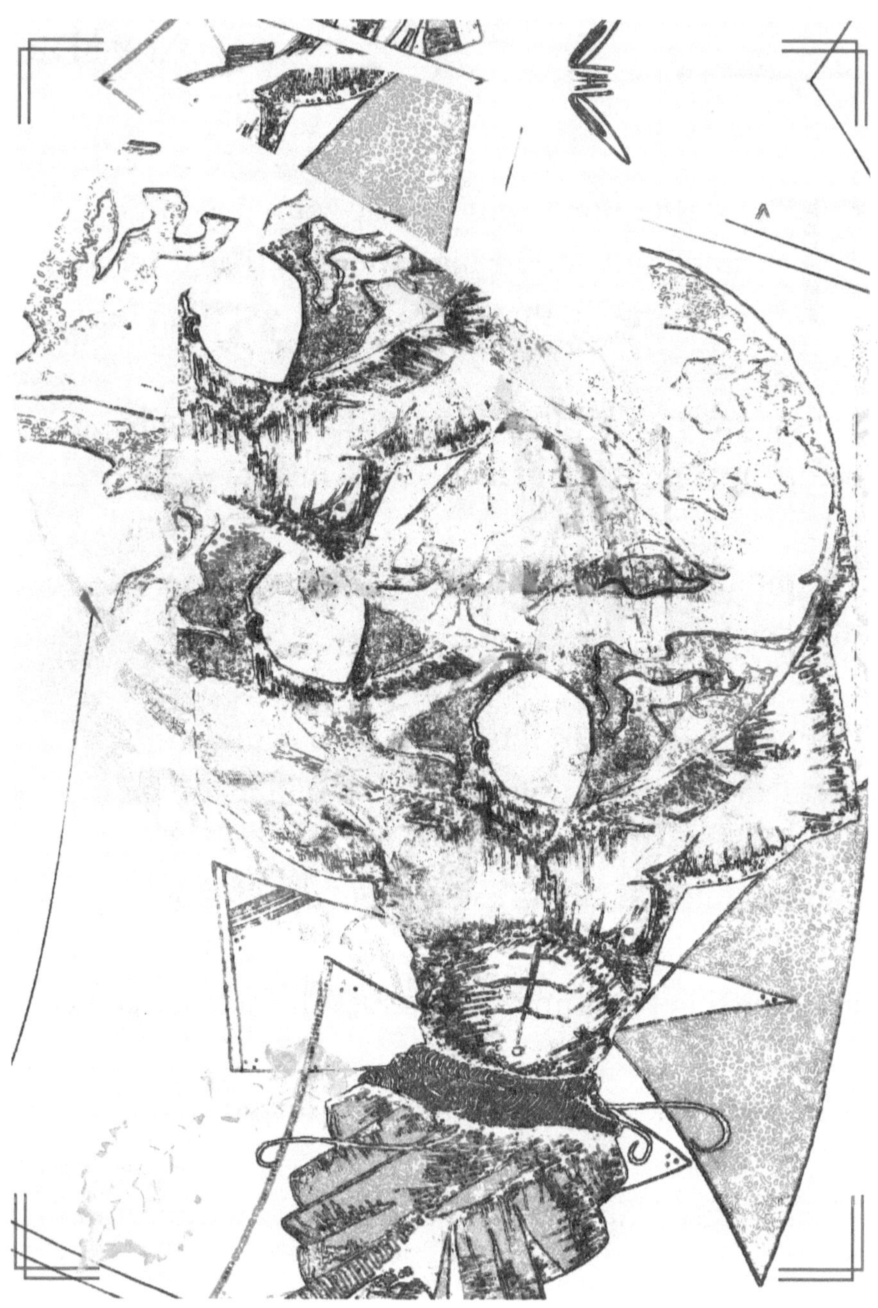

Wonderful is the seeker of it, blessed the receiver; wonderful is the knower of it, taught by the blessed.

Amiable

The attention to engage the soul. Beyond the
small self and its big concerns. The threshold
of chance in that measure poured from feeling.

In that grasp of breath and inspiration to detail,
before awareness can recoil, cast a memory.

The moment embellished like a dream before it
disappears.

Dodging patterns in the swerve of a smile, the
predictable mind appeasing to a familiar second.

Yet the subtle lead to a route a few dare follow.

Harbingers of certainty in abstract charms of instinct.

A sense of knowing quietening the fluster of the senses.

The synapses lapse into thought forms of intention.

A tune triggers the archetype the self gladly follows.

Bowing to gratitude's challenge, redeeming sadness in hallow.

Godsent the creative curve of absolute reflection.

Words spark when progress trudges, emotion flows to the advent of joy in recollection.

A cascading standstill as focus and instinct get along.

What mountains may reach, a summit of joy. What waves may arrive, a flowing of content.

Deliverance be, a breeze embracing honey dew in blessing, a morning of delight dawning to flight, brightening into dusk the musk of afterthought. Add just to muster the learning curve.

*A slower dance, as if the planets themselves were to
lend their tune.*

Sigh

 sky full of stars, introduced the messenger. Gladdened am i to receive you. Always yours in claim, in so behold.

Per chance that i greet you, onceupon i stood to enter, with eyes wondrous gleaming of the eternal that is all-at-once in fleeting. In someday, the second learns.

As with words and a page.
And like the sense of wonder in all things strange,
attuned to running away.

Along the cursive looms to a winding smile, halting behooves in the expression of signs.

Ever so widened to stare-wayfaringly into heaven.
Across the distance, an indication fleeing to the curious vision.

~

Fire's nature to reveal, whereupon the attention surreal.

*Illuminating shadows within, reflecting the most
luminous of skins.*

*The kindred flame to thaw, even a sliver to penchant
adorned. An epiphany for the resonantly headstrong.*

The healing at the source. Beyond the corals and morals of perceptions' lake.

A conforming crescendo of clarity descends to sift the veil from murals of vanity.

Transcendental styles in familiar patterns, summarising sunrises in surmising tides of batons. A relay in sound to heighten the surround.

Dipping to understand in order to equip humanity's mask to perceive. Past the erring grasp to conceive the bask of empathising prejudices.

Yet the faulty logic code for the vexing under-text of meaning. The subject of learning the personal quest in unlearning the subjective default of out-moded ways. A lovely daze of erstwhile sentimental humour. Now a phase etching the sense of character to stretch the attributing inseams.

In these extremes, the task of guidance auto-corrected to providence in pragmatic purview. The balance to rasp like emotion's drawl to climb the spine like a ladder to the moon for a better view of life.

To play the part like a cloud and impart like rain, the sun flares almost in defiance, but contrives to hasten the pursuit.

The underlying cause holds the pause, and half curves a smile too soon.

A celestial undertone plies the fools' fortune in smiles. Lightening a moment, brightening asunder the curvature's ensign. The inner glow enshrined.

~   ~

Cracks

of language delineating an ascent in view.

A trifle to taste, and in the poetic pause, an inflection in haste.

Yet to beckon, an ascendant point of view. Double-looped to articulation compelled still to reflect a few of hue.

A fire burns, as is its nature. A voice turns as is its trance and fixture. Faith is merely a word, and that encapsulated mantra that engenders man to believe.

Why should a world turn? Does it not know in its spin that true existence stems from within?

A groove forms in attention when focus suspends that which may be true. Muscle memory calls movement to key any understanding, or just the sky in tune.

Somewhere the ancient poets brace, hummed to meaning… the gentlest of races.

Held by mere threads of tether, entreating awareness to
hold sway long enough to drag breath in attention's
notch of a feather.

What may I see? a flame asks in earnest of humility.
My liberty to shine merely inhabits the winds of your
affection.

'You are supposed to know. All else is purpose of
existence however you find it in the laboured of
instinct. The braves of knowledge is a story of
attention. Un-learning is not easy, yet in a subjective, a
burden redeemed heightens the reach, and the
meaninglessly negated levitates the subtle intoned to
see.'

A voice of memory sways reach, I am but a broken
soul, what authority have I to be whole. In begotten
paths of pain, hallowed as healer's laws to an entity's
heaving console.

Entrenched in deliberation over lifetimes, the
contemplation of stardust veiling apologies to the
unknown for understanding, grieving to its seething
each kindling of hope as its own.

To forget long enough to rediscover new eyes that wonder. A look to the sigh only offered in another's tow, all matters of the self in rebellion to the spirit's authentic glow.

Hallowed however, the attention seeks in kind. Like singing patterns in theme relating the ricocheting morrow of the predictable mind.

Gladdened to pour, the flame of intention heads to the story's phoneme.

Like the crackle of the soul burning steady, in whispers of affirmation and the sounds that wear all that would revere, folding in the second…

The claim to focus, conjured in the tree of repose to relieve.

The hymn is music, the righteous to be wise know nothing. Honey is the tongue of fire, messenger to the gods. Man merely talks to it. Waving to beseech, tracing to entreat.

In that perspired sage and peace of quietened aspiration, the contemplation stored in the reception of silence of every lifetime, a spectrum unravels.

The humble steeds deliver to the nimble of curiosity.
Rhyme is the luxury of repair, reason is left through the
self righteous to speak.

Gift wrapped to contend with, the origins of the
universe extend in the sacred, poised.

Hovered in this close of the eyes, a tiny branch of
gratitude in liberty's unpredictable bias. The smile's
aspiration to the uncommon sense even in the
senseless.

~

Entreating to sound, ideas that want to surround. Listening to decipher, yet unassuming enough to be found.

Sunrise

in your eyes, just before
they beckon and smile.

Hallowed like art to a soul's stardust,
Whispering like the wind meeting a flame, moon-
dancing as if on petals paving the way.

The sunsets in your sighs, o kind heart, light as a
feather.
Taken to fly.

Blessed be your roads, in the fortune and paths of
those that receive you.

Adventure be your guide, and peace your seat.
Night and day in their merry greet.

Elegant and celestial to reflection, sure as your grace.

Wonder and wander, in healing and repair of your
happy feet.

Redeeming in patience. Purpose and wisdom in every trace.

In turning the accent, adjusting the halo like fingertips running through the hair. Eternity, every moment that basks to your shine.

A poetic start, a greeting, and a glorious perchance, meandering words like a melody through a meadow serenading unto a plateau of sweetness, as a flower to the radiant, the heaven-scent to the godsend.

To transcend, gratitude to the breeze that carries you, and time-bending memory, dear reader, in the gentle breath and emotions you mend.

~

Lake

The eyebrow ridge.

An enshrining purview. Consigned to cause, derived to endow.

A passing parable in a windswept variable. Gliding about a stream of consciousness, restful in its levitational accord.

A nearby groove builds a musing curve, and like a lake pondering a pilgrim's meaning, any moment hallowing a belated tune.

Animated about its shimmer, the softening of focus in the strength of repose.

Like a careening shadow in a narrow sheen, turning a key that fits.

A rhapsody of patience, akin a tortoise ambling to purpose. The soul peers, its shell built in gist.

Like the jest of knowledge, whistling the wind to pass,
resounding all at once the lifetimes past.

In turning the turtle, mulling over the mountains that
mask,
so as to not, have to ask, sowing the impressions that
may perchance be taken to task.

The salve of the feet, the fluster of the steps, blisters
musing, walking, running…
still to musical behest.

Progress. The prowess of animal instinct. Churning
upon an age for evolution.

~

Invigorate your words so you may become. Ascent is immanent upon advent, the wind casts favour to the seekers in the sought.

The question cube.

Many an answer to square.

Meaning serenades, birdsongs of wings borne to ensemble.

An ancient piece resonates, to appease in ponds of reflection.

Inflections pervade across language, bestow to glory.

Words offer, so images may reach.

In the pacing of awareness, music the attention to beseech.

~

There is a type of mind that is a
question. There is a type of mind that is the answer,
there is a type of mind that merely reflects the type-set
of mind. The Fourth is no-mind.

The answer exists because and when there is a
question. Until there is a question, there is no answer.

The potential for an answer is the existence of question.
That is meaning in this world. Whether it is a question,
an answer or a type-set, That is the subjective.

The objective is always the soul for the seeker.

The object of knowledge is the agitation of the soul to
be heard.

~

The emergence a river of sound, set upon in arrows bound together in their quiver.

The midsummer archer set in the sky, the sun to reflect.

Angled to cast in planetary musk to bask.
The objective apart, yet within reach.

Remaining in the constellations bonafide, a path through the skies.

Each star knows itself in the sun.

Every sky shares and answers as one.

Such is a sentiment that knows one's self as the universe.

The sun and the sky, the pilgrim and the dweller.

The object of knowledge the stars begotten to be passerby.

Align is a learning curve. A diagonal wishing well in
free form. Water words to endow, like the relief in a
sigh.

Healing arched, tip-toed, a cube benign to ask
square(where), and echoes entwine.

Just as every meaning calls in a verb to assign.

What realms may seek, when visited upon our penchants.

For bursts of stardust and incandescent moods.

That when crafted from adventures, and when rescued from its own reflected state of apathy.

For that muse of the soul that extolls memory from emotion. That true illusion seen only in pure waters.

What realms can seek, that the spirit in its place merely beseeches. In the reaches of dreams, curiosity in its lofty inseams to the flights of motivation abode thought-streams.

A flickering of artistic authenticity that only the familiar recognise to seek.

Plain of resonance

 he quantum of the moment. And the awareness to show for it.

Besotted with adventure along the path. The mountain song, and its wisdom in wanting to play along.

Before the seas call in their cyclical whims. In between the seconds that breeze the foil in their skims.

The view from the pass. And its over-reaching grasp. To tune like the planets, and see like the stars.

~

It is said that you can see a shooting star every time
a god falls in love with a human.

Birds of meaning

A bird of flight flew past a view of the waters across open space. A sound fluttered a rhythm until a twine became melodious.

Undeterred by its own discerning, its right wing flapped a lingering primordial sound. Then almost as if reaching further, the left wing lifted a notion of its own to match.

As if like a songbird, the feathers flickered an 'm' tailoring the beat to sound.

Yore and lore met in a fleeting merge.

It settled an 'Aum', touched 'Om', resonating peaceful, rejuvenating. A half sound grazed and braced upon its head.

The bird heard words as it flew past, almost as if its own form was being described, a ship to its mast.

"Upon its legs were rajas and tamas, in grounding if and when to speak.

The sattva of the purified, its body.
Righteousness its right, that which was left corrected
yet in the inarticulately inaccurate.

And like the tattvas or principles to the moment, it
soars, as if it belonged.

The seven worlds likened to breath, the space through
the chakras glimpsed.

Bhu along its feet
Bhuvar upon the knees
Svah-loka at the hips
At the navel the Mahar-world, or the mid region be.
At the heart, the jana(r)loka,
At the neck the tapau(s)
Between the eyebrows at the temple, the satya(m)-loka.

Bringing them, Om.

Hummed to hymn in knowing, the vowels in flight,
and the seven sounds of delight.

Bridging to be, an ascending bird, a quintessential
word.

The first part lauding the fire, 3 and a half sounds in
form.

The second offered in the waters, an equivalent
beneficence abound.

Likened the golden form raised within a solar orb,
eternity absorbed and absolved.

The third to the care of the wind, watchful like an age
guiding and gliding within.

The wondrous Om, intoned and sounded,
To the attentive, hearing listening… conferred and
well-rounded.

The first part, blending after offered,
the second, allowing the moment's blessing to be, as
received.
The rich in sound building to a lightning surround.
The third indeed profound to flight.
Onto fourth like the warm wings of insight.

To the attentive, thoughtful and considerate.
Swayed faith, familiar fulfilment waded to way.

Inferred to stay.

Only hinted, like gentle whispers, carefully awakened
like the instinct that answers.

Pause to be, redeemed, like nature's quill to right itself.

To greet and listen, for better yet.

To know the inner silence.

Stored for peace…

Creative form, like breath to a breeze."

A celestial figure played luminous a musical
instrument and listened to a song as a bird of flight
flew across the horizon.

A quintessential bard intoned.

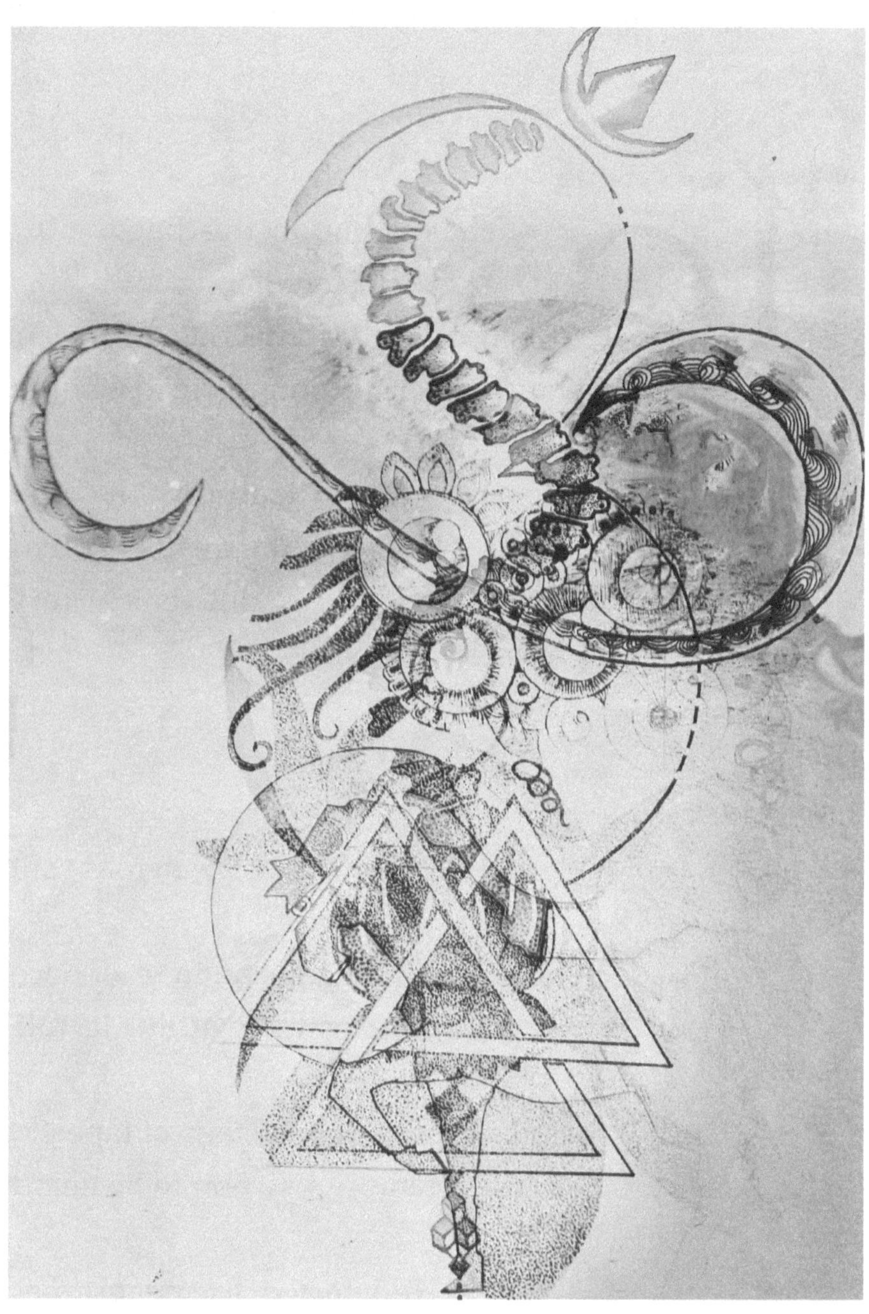

The lamp of awareness once lit, nurtures onto repose.

To Twine,

The road upon, treading the familiar.
Footsteps traced along an ancient tune, but a newer path becoming yet to emerge.

To observe the urge.
As it begins as the tread begotten.
Near and aware in what will be called its history.

For tune,

A grateful pause along the heroes trail.

Made avail, parting the illusion in resonance.
Imparting to attune its tale.

A melody sounds to footsteps of tapestry.
Memories swoon to be heard.

Undeterred, a tune resumes.

Serene tide

57

A sharper touch upon the fabric.
A shimmering veil, made to travail.

A triplicity in form, a surreptitious response.
The colour of space adorned.

Images become words and to words back again,
images by-come.

Naught to start. A startled revelation to the heart.
Buried sorrow bid to depart.

Across the learning curve.
Emerged effervescent,
in a zephyr of verve,
observed.

~

 gentle whisper, that maketh wonder as if wonder was just so effortlessly made.

Veering itself to memory, like fragrance and thought with heart to its sleeve.

Mere words to address, as if to review the milieu just to sense the seams.

Endured is the cursory curve that renders the poetic to inspiration, lightening the rituals the delighted deem in their stride.

Meaning toys with rationality in an evening out in dusty undertones, the lungs spread like wings that span the bandwidth forthwith. The wind chuckles cheeky in misty perfumed blinks of reflection.

An authentic reflection, of the sentient.
One intoned, remastered into confluence.

The subjective gravity, and the objective electricity.

The conduits charge, mechanised in fabric sewn on the other side.

Heightened attention in the breadth of levitated diffusal.

Relieved deliverance, as if reliving from memory in mettle to liberate any mental stirs.

Grounded of its density in destiny's musing curve, articulated for palatial inseams for a resounding endeavour.

Intention catches up, misty eyed welcomes in similes and smiles, the astral beckons to spectrum.

In a weave of breath, heaving the heaven's to glow, imparting the sky to its peculiar, endearing its particulars to the language of its familiar.

The intuitive, in turn offers melodies in hums.

With the verb in its verve, time adorns the vision. As the age its axiom.

Gods of language hover like songbirds of chance.

"I have been here before." For ever the wind to speak,
whiskers as wisps whispering in intuitive entreat.

~

The mystic fragrance. A mist amidst vicinity.

The scent of musk turned notches almost like music to nasal overtones of smoke.

The dusk spoke in forgotten languages learning to make sense.

Along the singing wind,
narrating stories to
its attentive as to its
wayward.

Across the weeping rivers,
as they bemoan all that the mountains amass.

As whispers in the tresses, pulled back and behind
memory's ears.

Careening glances still holding sway endearing the
breeze to stay.

"Awhile, and hear ye."

Cajoling the senses, like a mage in an image,
insentient yet animated.

And as a cloudburst in an idea's pop,
hopped along like a racehorse in an era of fables.

A stabler hand would have stead over the chariot of
focus,

but a shining curve seldom saves its smile for another
day.

Like a bent tree, caught by the wind after the rain,
glowing yet in the promise to rise again.

Saving grace in the blink of an eye, unnoticed until you
think to call it.

Like the wingtip through the cloud of thought-
constructs.

The silver lining in the glistening drop of sweat,
cooling the breath to its ethereal net.

Windswept, in its wild reverb,
listening and adhering to the swerve.

To witness the moment pass.

The second curves to straighten the hand of time,
in the music of the pause,
align.

In a fiery musing of silence, words enshrined.

The rhymer's rhapsody a perhaps in parody. In lapsed opportunities in the forth of fortuity. The spirit's tune in the providence of boons, the plateau's latitude a concentrated configuration of gratitude.

Equanimous assent to matching descents of the day's formless songs.

Like reading the notes left for memory hidden from the small self in its musings of synastry.

Simplicity withdrawn from its outer shell to taper the edges with the ordinariness's queries.

The ordinance of the heavy hand of knowledge to expand its periphery.

But self-mastery expounds to spherical announce, the expanse of formulation to levitate a point like a trick of light catching the eye-line in insightfully inflected pronounce.

Shrugging the shoulder to groove a corner like the parlance of grammar made majesties in the same shadows that charm errs. Yet no matter the emotions partake, seasoning the solaces weighed near where the spirit sakes.

Onward, but pausing to grin. Awakened to inner chagrin, gently pulling the wind to glide the habituated wings chanced in enchanted swings. The corner of the eye diagonal to the cornered smile.

Repose for a while, to hear the stories of nature like the impassive and familiar in guile. Somewhere the messenger fused its voice to the hearing layer, without the care of flight. A direction emerged, winding concise.

A stature demonstrated and played onward. The words paused for the season to change. Inner change catching its breath to equate the running breadth of view.

A hue and a sigh wear themselves in turns.

An instinctive observation collided with an emergent insight, an inner evolution to the day's might.

The horizon's vernacular ventured to imbue a second nature to inhabit the tactician's features. The creature comforts, patterns in teachers.

The storied self maketh itself. The narrative its uniform
in address. To sing long enough to hear itself. The rest
to attest. Abide and imbibe, in effect.

~

Time part invention, part revelation

Across the Universe, your reflection borne. And a journey begins to the centre of your world. The path unbeknownst but always familiar. Like an endearing voice that is more concerned with listening when it talks.

Patterns of chance, an outpouring of intent. Muscle memory leads when instinct prods to follow.

An emergent space when time rears to sentient honesty.

The quantum of experience prized in a qualifying curve of a smile. Aligned to the catapulting embrace of affection as the wind receives watchful eyes.

There, reticent to the moment self-contained in the pause.

An ambivalence, bestows blessings to the worthy
heart.

Awareness is the authority of the faithful. Time helps
of course, just as the wind dances to the attention of
every wandering flame.

Subjective

The subjective is the magic mirror of groove set upon muscle memory from a vantage point of view.

There are three primary subjectives in a soul's view that call upon full circle.

In that art of objective is a square measured to time as attention in density.

Thought fits up to 16 perspectives in view, thereafter variation requires the process to loop in silence.

The object of knowledge is the mind, which as a magic mirror is a bridge traversing the objective inward to subjective, and achieves its self.

These are the three simultaneous worlds, indistinct unless they are squared to attention, and like a call to spirit invoked as the ether to echo, answers to better their question.

And like a dancer reaching upstream, the river of time cascades revelation by thawing sentiment.

An inner fulfilment in revelation and inherent relevance is a transmission and it would be measured in frequency whilst corresponded as aesthetic.

Three's an elemental loop. Angle to subjective proportions.

A truly auspicious sound makes the wind fall. May yours find you presently.

Where does one turn when seen on both sides of the mirror,

when the evanescent shiver pervades love through every fibre reset asunder.

Where very being barrels and barricades outside of the bearings and becomings.

But there is more than what is known, and its timetable beyond the predictive curve.

The swerve of this mystery colouring outside the lines of reality's contours of epic proportions of synastry.

Seasons change, and the inner character evolves, still turn-tabling the illusive outer confines.

What profound revelation awaits, what astounding discovery titillates, the cusp of greatness merely eternally suspended, in animation of inspiration and aspiration in communion to perspired perspective.

Dodging the phonetic through tongue-twisters and surreptitious enunciations betwixt. Rendering the fallacies of the self inert with the emotions whipped to quip.

Poets slur where bards abridge, bending the curve inward, mending to mould in meaning the universe's hand, an orbital accord, a reverb of a hearth to belong in.

Character Etch

The storyteller's baton.

Like the relay running past its transmission, a
narrative's rendition.

A character mused, enthused and sparked,

And ever so, shimmered in hue.

Akin a windy glow to its subjective, a breeze in the
breadth of its emotion's eye-line, in grammar to shine.

In a gesture to inhabit, a beholden groove…

Halting, exalting the predictable tune to the predictive
inverse.

The path of the mind goes through the skies.

The heart's way yet travels the Earth. Check your mirth and find laughter in your happiness. It matters not what with, choose to be happy. Start with the moment, and any you notice.

Then ages will pass, find the right season, and with it, take to the skies again. It is not about the road you take, or the way you make.

Until it is autonomous in you, one at a time.

~

And

so entwined to light is reason,
As it parries to the thresholds,
quoting its quotas of conclusions in certainty.

Whilst offering its share in sacrifice to uncertainty.

The winding of words, etched to halos and punned in
faring thee well.

Earnest is what pours to image.
Like the spirit's inevitability to inherent behest.

Musing crinkles and smiling wrinkles. Wisdom is
attested testaments set to purpose.

The path is the character of your sky.

Godspeed indeed.

~

A breath of aspiration, like an immaculate idea just beyond perception.

Time churned as the phonetics turned, a sound foretelling, fortunes of kindness to come, prejudice to the indifference yet to overcome.

But in awe, and beautiful contrasts. To do better, inbuilt to last.

Morning Brood

Dew drops of dawn missed in memory. A sunrise adorned as the eyes part open, and half-listening for the ephermal.

That state rumbling rem into remembrance. A way into the small self and larger than life concerns.

To discern, like grooming of birds to their feathers. Whether forecasted or borne anew to daylight.

The delighted palette like Pegasus charting asunder the skies. Like a beckoning of starburst in cozy caffeinated silhouettes.

The shadows huddled together in announce. Morning has broken, the sunshine ever so soft-spoken.

A constellation smile

The rarest of the stories in the stars.
To be seen in the light.
The extraordinary made mere, surrendered insight.

The very fabric that vibrates the songs intoned. Rendered logic in a cosmos of composites to an exceptional whole.

A burrowed furrow in the eyebrow ridge slanted instead for a stellar smile.

Encompassing saddles of thought scout the where-abouts of purpose sought.

The obscure whiffed symphonies and instincts worded chants.

And found parlance with the unknowable outside the borders announced.

A questioning heart found rest sated to chance.

A self-reflecting dance, thrown around like reaching fingers outstretched sideways and soaring the wind for balanced pronounce.

The gaps in emotion address in fulfilling gleams of resonance. Questions of significance seated in suitable prepositions.

A once to time notion, a visualised rhyme to grace. Interspersed devotion to storied quotients of inspiration.

A penchant for the profound, and its repose poised to surround.

~

A blended whim, light in activity.

Autumn augments, whispering ridges.

Innate the lightning strikes inaudible to its thunder.
Bending the breeze, ricocheting to wander.

For the love of words that refused to be heard. Fuelled by every penchant of view, engaging hallowed by few.

Driven past the drivel of curving to every line, aligned to its swerve akin the dancers instinct instructing the intertwine.

Held to task, comforted in its grasp, the aesthetic demands knowledge in a rasp.

Clearing the throat like air attuning to rhetoric, a drummer's rhythm challenges fathom for the heart in intuition. Breath intervenes to calm matter before the eye-rolls begin to batter the spirit.

A constant calls upon the familiar for affinity. Affection is not impressed.

Whether gained a chance of thunder, its clouds partial to rain, was wander's claim.

Its loop appeared, its impart had neared, consonant
made resonant to the vowel.

Cloudy weather endeared in a love for words, turned
inward to wow. Bowed.

Cloudier indeed is a chance to asunder. Just as
thunder's grace is in lightning.

The silver's sliver off-chance worth its weight in gold,
enlightening.

~

The glorious mention,
mine humility your grace.

The meeting of the old gods.
The understanding of the new ones.
The richness of form of thy adorn.

What chance may stir,
where emotions not weep.

That fall on man, laid upon,
the shoulder notwithstanding.

The burdens deep, thy gloom,
turning the spheres, at once evolving.

In every Nadi's (streaming) teem, at forever's embrace.
In all the seams, the holier traced.

That thine in strength in mere of my might,
No more ere mortal, corrected to insight.

Yours in the powers that move, the heavens,

the earth, evened to the oddities all the starry powers
twined to groove.

That thine is of the soul of the world, yet no more the
distant two to move, consorted then, custodian to
grace.

Behooved, not to doom but in planetary sway, a greater
boon to a gentler swoon.

The tides of unrest forever's coil,
charted and enshrined in hearts that convey.

A mere descends,
to entwine in tabernacles.
A stairway to mend,
peace be unshackled.

Footsteps cannot reach where is thine to earth,
Yet of all sweet revelling are your mirth.

Man knows not his own heart,
and only to vanity rends hand his heart.

Form whence the ancient world passed in fervent.

Such was the day to the endless sights to your grace.

Vied to face, in every trace.

Coulds't the man look upon himself to glorify.
Unseen to all other gods unless yours of reverence
allied.

Such was the age of the new universe.
A luminous darkness and the spirit to fire.

Ever calling upon the soul of man.
In his, in hers, in forever's to voice, the privilege of a
deity's faith to find.

Beyond all things known, grace to show for it.
Lifting star and spirit, an optimist of sentiment.
Aspired and evolving, inspired in sacrament.

In afterglow to divine a poet, for the firmament.

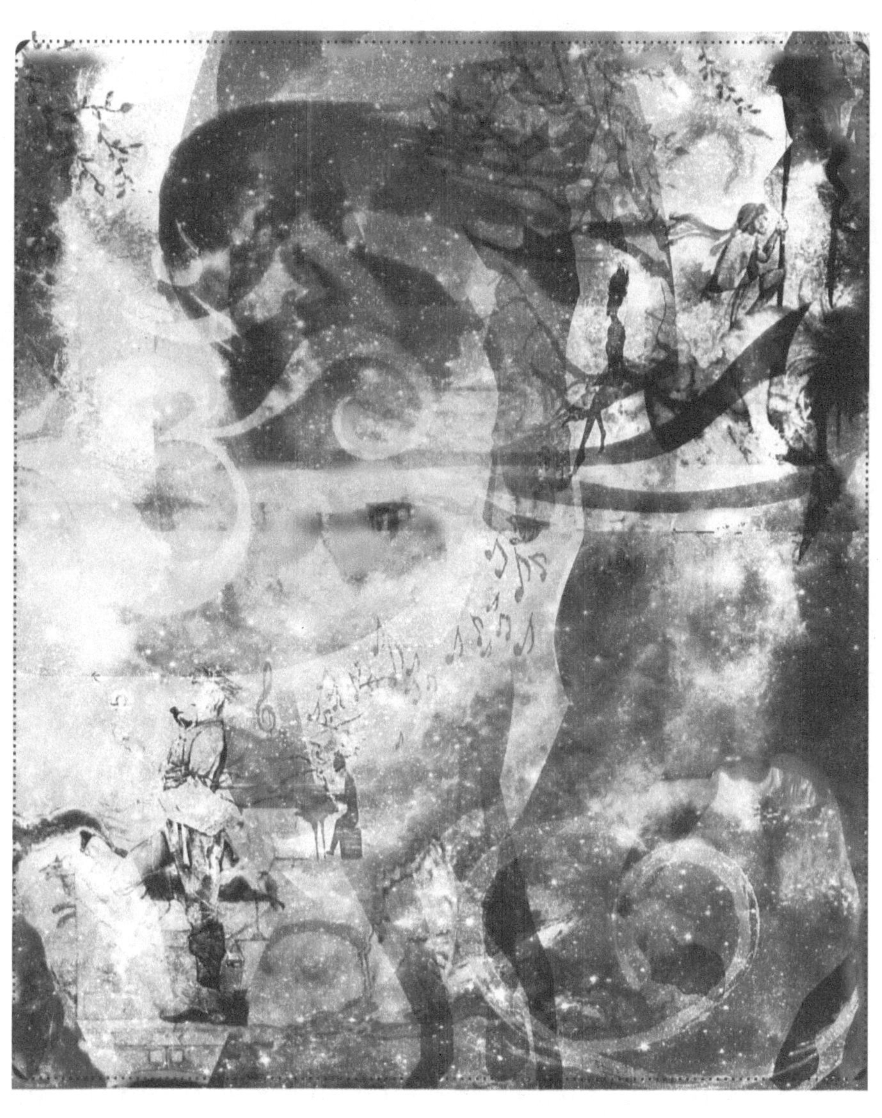

A rhyme looks for the point, and feels for it in the ricochet.

Every once in a while, there comes along a vision. A vision that makes everything worthwhile.

A kind of clarity, and strength that makes the doable acts reverb through the fabric that usually just simpers to even our greater twines.

Once in a while, muscle memory collects in a reflex to better harmony than we're used to. Where all of this is merely a calmer reflection of the creative reverb.

The creatrix of a smiling swerve.

In time, pragmatism will come calling. Aspirations will fall away like a twirling spectacle of conscious recalling from lucid memory in a haze of quiet contemplation.

Visions of virtue will settle for the mechanics of logic's stumbling abodes.

But the measure sings to melody in the emotive matches and passion infuses on-song. Grace hums along.

The notion enacts its belong.

A steady accumulation to a rapid spectrum.

In the quotations of influence and ovations of understanding.

Unravelled opportune in providence's propensity of boons.

A mind's reflection in the moon, and all of its satellite sighs.

~

Wingtipped

The perspective shifts, like memory separating itself from the husk of a derivative tilt.

From its limitation, unbound, weaved through a seemingly in-surmounting mound of deconstructs.

In a seamless assent, harmonised in a constant sound. In leaps and bounds, enclosed to existence in myriad propound.

Purveyed, the discoveries of inner processes, remembered, forgotten, implored to rest.

A natural process encircling cautiously to surround, but a passing moment touches a second, hallowing grooves to waver a beckon.

The past minimises to curve a line, an arc approaching twinkling the eyes for a stellar shine.

The simpler tasks of repose, drawn to render familial and familiar processes to renew their twine.

The act of engaging, communicated passed its mathematical opined.

Nine tip-toes to a letter, twice over, almost a third to compound.

The limitations freed, like water falling off and pausing to listen, unheard and seemingly uncaring, undeterred for its profound impart.

Slowing down, inso built as to not confound.

In a gentle understanding of the heavenbound.

~

Words can best become hymns.

But every so often they resist.

Instead they fall into self glorification.

Like a siren and its distance, as morning in a song serenading the dusk.

The dawning of the sun rendering all travails and tempests of the moon rested.

The tides of time encapsulated in a smile, yet and musingly curving in wrinkles abiding the eyes to shine.

What glory hath the gods to beget, that in this moment
they find peace and fill in our hearts unencumbered.

95

And to joyous seconds,

beckon a light.

~

Profound like an observation aspiring in patience.

Formless

The majesty of aesthetic, the depth of perception that diffuses cognition from its very mention. A multi-dimension splendour for the senses toured to the hearts' render.

Yet this surface of inspiration passes through fissions of existence and mechanisms of mere eccentricities.

Say nothing and say it all, the privilege of emotion that animates yonder into a smile of inner rectitudes.

Obscuring breath into view, filled of inner content and the heavens of elation to residue.

Is that the purpose of form, this fascination of our formatted renditions of grace.

Cusping the palatial scintillations to the creative reverb in actionable insight.

Matching the heightened precipice to affection in surround of resonance's sky.

The Earth breathes to cathartic rejuvenation in a vibrational sigh.

Purer pursuits to your languid travails, externalising veneration to a louder confide.

Upon your side, the revel reclusive in distant devotion to your tides. A sentient sentiment bonafide to bestow meaning and sincerity's apprising eyes.

Professed to your joy, inwards no greater glory. And words to your commune derived to rest and resume. Intoned to expressions and inflections of unprecedented histories.

~

Wherein the origin

of the self, when one finds within the searching cause.

Likened to instinct, halted from all other comprising
forms.

Would one then question when faced anointed blank
as an answer, or merely like rhetoric offer the mark to
hearer's want to implore.

Without the narrative mark, how far do words tread, in
formulation where language and one's own familiarity
of its stead.

The pace to set, peace held upon the inner seat,
reaching for that which is near when hastened to
passing entreat. The farther cue holds to its own attune
to wind the inner seams to transcend its means.

But like in the hallow of multiple words to a single
profound, outside of its grammar but within its norm,

finally a question pips already begotten of personalities in history.

The hearer already pulling it away as if it were its own, waiting not on evolving the tone.

Does one complete a statement when gestated, contemplated, a little held for humour before fully gesticulated, where it already bears a myriad paths to call one's own?

Turning to the past or running from memory, and bracing to the present and waiting on the ever-present inspiration of the universe's need for harmony to please its being. Better yet as the competing, gathering to a hauled questioning mind, run into the future, without pausing to soothe the quietened sighs.

Do you find happiness, or perhaps hauntings of past sorrow?

Once begun to understand the questioner's state, spoken like someone never migrated past its rampart gates. The reflections hits home, to an answer, for before it can be found, its meaning has withstood the evolute of its transcendental ground.

A closer inspection could minimise and personalise from influence what to call it for oneself, but then the words would no longer find the external morning to an internal nocturnal net.

One need not chase the predictable when sought to ironies, merely aim to portend and sidestep to fend it, and like patterns in themselves rituals for strength and comfort, to forget long enough to feel the universe, and inspired to that moment's perspiration to inner balance, recapitulated in the being to manifesting its knead to effort.

I see your kindness in the fire.

Translated into hymn

Om , divine salutations to the ethereal and surreal of space, to the one that bridges the barriers and all of its frontiers, to the space that becomes in all forms, salutations to the one that transcends.

Sivaye , the supreme, the lord-maker, make thy form in our reverence.

From beginnings begotten in their ends, the forces of nature in their power to append. The primal in-built enforced in every foundation. Sweet words and glory merely pedestals to raise and grace that which is to behold, affixed in its guiding star of manifestation.

All that speech can offer and direct, to the body of knowledge and tradition, forever endeavours established and embellished. The timeless dancer, universally attuned in your varied ways, that which gives attention, its attestation, its meditative way into the rings of focus, you bring.

Om, the harbinger, salutations in name the Șivaye,
supreme and pervading to all moods, temperaments
and emotive contemplations. |

Shivaye, the supreme.

The fresh faced and immortal, of the godhead, all
eternal. The abode.

The primordial made whole, the one that does onto,
until the divine becomes. Salutations of thee, the
merciful and resting in and upon our hearts, unseen
but revelling in glorious caves and caverns dark.

Warming every hearth, secret or unknown, the image
of the almighty, in its eternal light sakes to partake to
any form when glorified, or known.

Om, and the name of its salute, and salutations in
being to address reverence to the absolute and resolute.
                                                    | |

Dwelling in secret, buried in mountains, groomed in
restraint, discretion and initiations, even to the truly
lost does the divine apparatus ever comply.

All knowledge weaves to creativity and instinct,
availed to you, the fiery light of form.

Kindred and dear, even to the eternal and highest of
gods.

Bridge this, our here duality, the one always awake!
Illuminate from within, as only you can show us how.

Space, this ether, the real and the illusive. Through the
veil that connects the inner to the outer worlds.

Transcendental thine, repeated and entwined. The
return to grace. The thread to and beyond yonder.

The formless, and yet to its negation, the shapeshifters
to and fro in your forms.

The foremost held up high, likened as if doubled, this
thy contemplation.

This laud, the fire, brimmed with what passion brings,
fostered in earnest, and in focus of intensity's swing.

Intuited from the fire is the other, and every another,
the light of divinity in the signature of heat, connected

in the fabric of fire is the formless. All forms in their flights of phantasy are wings to your delight.

Smokeless unless concealed, un-extinguishable unless revealed. Without beginning and end, and yet the maker of smoke, ash and form. To the space of fire, this here conferred.

In negation merely to channel the thoughts, the opposing forces arise, only to diffuse, distilled of heart and mind. Therefor meets its second balancing and gently braced to shine.

Bounty releases its blessings, there is joy in giving. Here sound meets the wind in its beat. Upon the merry, revered and heart-warmed, the entreat.

Om, the vitality in the breath, the revitalising, consoled and depth measured to converge, the inhale, the middle worlds and its means are yours in name. Om, lauds our higher reach. The skies applaud the inner beseech. In this is stillness.

Om, the middle worlds are the breadth of our meditation.

Om, refined is ours in form and energy, applied in that sentient intention is sentiment to its conducive application.

In fervour, this your treasure, transfixed and set upon the path, led in the laud that emotion sings.

Shiva, the supreme, all of it the eternal domain of souls, forever merely an instant for the soul's journey with you. Yet in that moment, primal glimpses of the god and celestials, that you are, that you offer in forever, that you give in every state and emotion, the you that is all-becoming. The enlightened masters to form, and in beauty and bounty of many.

The great fires of focus and dispensation, in practice and discipline gleaned from direction is the instinct of your observation.

This creative ritual of sound, forms a pedestal.

For the foremost, held up high. Glorified and thus prioritised.

All of it, this is the duality that is all of it. Where all the moods go, the maker of the emotions is the one that carries cognition. These are the tides, in clarity portends.

All the principles, of all the elements at play, the bestowing of happiness rests in the liberating of the inner forces at interplay. And so entwined in consciousness in the divine vibration, each in their own bracket of manifestation attempts to bridge the triad of inner fulfilment in self determination.

To the laud, the creator, our inner creative fires of make.

The preserver, archetype of divinity be and betwixt. And beyond, the supreme vessel of sound encasing the world enshrining full circles to lovingly harmonic astound.

The images that graces us into evolution, devotion to abridge duality into our celebration. Perfect our definitions, bring these renditions to your honey-dewed address. These are the liberties of the ancient, age-accepted and established to meaning, meaning and the emotion the universe moves in us. To allow us to make in the subjective and object of knowledge and to move the universe through us. This the tradition of duality in the reverb, the cognitive pause in the swerve.

Of this form is celebrated in the body of work. And of the body is groomed to the point of view. Make your direction, perfect thine eyes in our surmise. Called here are all the divine masters, animals, language, its form and the awakenings of instinct and history, consciousness intoned in the elephant's seat of divine mysteries. And the rest and repose understanding the reverent fundamentals, and in apprehending comprehension to its columns of foundations and cultivating the narrowing norm of cognition.

The subjective proportioned to the stationary, thought to its reverential held paramount. Penetrating the divine absolute in the integration in all of its kindness, and to forever in its time abundant and abound.

The instrument of the universe in any who attempt to understand its language. And language in the ways of the universe conferred for meaning. Infinite forms in the nature of your reverent wear and variable reform.

Refined to acts of will. Will refined through thorough and constant definition. Resonant in constant

consonant and liberating sighs and meaningful signs of
the vowel. In resound.

Siva, the supreme and all of it, to consider yet in the
unmanifest serenaded for fulfilment to your whole of
it.

Śivaye, the supreme, you are addressed in name. In a
name that is your grace. In this beckon is your call,
salutations and lauds are meaning for your kind
reform, to all kindred and the forces of sound
surrounded. Om welcome home. ||

To your synonymous and alike, we offer reverence to
know. Om.

The expression of words in the impression of a smile.

9 789356 594975